P9-CDF-292

DK READERS

Level 3

Level 4

A Note to Parents

DK READERS is a compelling program for beginning readers, designed in conjunction with leading literacy experts, including Dr. Linda Gambrell, Distinguished Professor of Education at Clemson University. Dr. Gambrell has served as president of the National Reading Conference, the College Reading Association, and the International Reading Association.

Beautiful illustrations and superb full-color photographs combine with engaging, easy-to-read stories to offer a fresh approach to each subject in the series. Each DK READER is guaranteed to capture a child's interest while developing his or her reading skills, general knowledge, and love of reading.

The five levels of DK READERS are aimed at different reading abilities, enabling you to choose the books that are exactly right for your child:

Pre-level 1: Learning to read
Level 1: Beginning to read
Level 2: Beginning to read alone
Level 3: Reading alone
Level 4: Proficient readers

The "normal" age at which a child begins to read can be anywhere from three to eight years old. Adult participation through the lower levels is very helpful for providing encouragement, discussing storylines, and sounding out unfamiliar words.

No matter which level you select, you can be sure that you are helping your child learn to read, then read to learn!

LONDON, NEW YORK, MUNICH,
MELBOURNE, AND DELHI

To Lia Xiushun Leonard

Series Editor Deborah Lock
U.S. Editor John Searcy
Art Editor Gemma Fletcher
Production Editor Siu Chan
Production Pip Insley
Jacket Designer Mary Sandberg

Reading Consultant
Linda Gambrell, Ph.D.

First American Edition, 2008
08 09 10 11 12 10 9 8 7 6 5 4 3 2 1
Published in the United States by DK Publishing
375 Hudson Street, New York, New York 10014

DK books are available at special discounts when purchased in bulk for
sales promotions, premiums, fund-raising, or educational use.
For details, contact:
DK Publishing Special Markets
375 Hudson Street
New York, New York 10014
SpecialSales@dk.com

A catalog record for this book is available
from the Library of Congress.

ISBN: 978-0-7566-3753-8 (Paperback)
ISBN: 978-0-7566-3752-1 (Hardcover)

Color reproduction by Colourscan, Singapore
Printed and bound in China by L. Rex Printing Co. Ltd.

The publisher would like to thank the following for their kind
permission to reproduce their photographs:
(Key: a-above; b-below/bottom; c-center; l-left; r-right; t-top)
Alamy Images: AA World Travel Library 14br; Dennis Cox 21b;
Ian Dagnall 20; D. Hurst 19br; Lou Linwei 31; Neil McAllister 21cr;
Mediacolor's 29cr; Sdbchina 33; Dave Stamboulis 24b; Ray Thrupp/
Agency Adams Picture Library 27br; Liu Xiaoyang 6. **Corbis:** Diego
Azubel/epa 23; Louis Laurent Grandadam 13; Dallas and John
Heaton/Free Agents Limited 3, 10-11; So Hing-Keung 42cb;
Alex Hofford/epa 37tr; Andrew K/epa 37b; Wolfgang Kaehler
9tr; Jason Lee/Reuters 41cb; Danny Lehman 11br; Liu Liqun 22bl;
Gideon Mendel 30t; Redlink 4crb, 24c; Michael Reynolds/epa 46;
Keren Su 7clb, 7crb, 35; Swim Ink 14tl; Robert Wallis 34b; Xinhua/
Xinhua Photo 44br, 45; Michael S. Yamashita 42tl. **DK Images:**
The British Museum 9tl (brush); Pitt Rivers Museum, University
of Oxford 12br. **Getty Images:** AFP 15t; Frederic J. Brown/AFP
15br; Cancan Chu 22tl; Alexander Hassenstein/ Bongarts 22br;
Liu Jin/AFP 30br; Minden Pictures/Gerry Ellis 38; Guang Niu
47t; Photographer's Choice/Frans Lemmens 28-29; Stephen
Shaver/AFP 36. **Interactive Visualization Lab/iVizLab:** 43cr.
PunchStock: Corbis/Redlink 19t; Digital Vision 8tl.
Jacket images: *Front:* **Corbis:** Mao Chen/epa.
All other images © Dorling Kindersley
For further information see: www.dkimages.com

Discover more at

www.dk.com

Contents

DK Readers

Welcome to China

Written by Caryn Jenner

DK Publishing

China today

Welcome to China. This ancient nation is now home to more people than any other country. One-fifth of all the people in the world live here. That's a population of 1.3 billion people—one billion more than the United States.

Chinese flag

| China | Zhōngguó [jung-gwo] | 中国 |

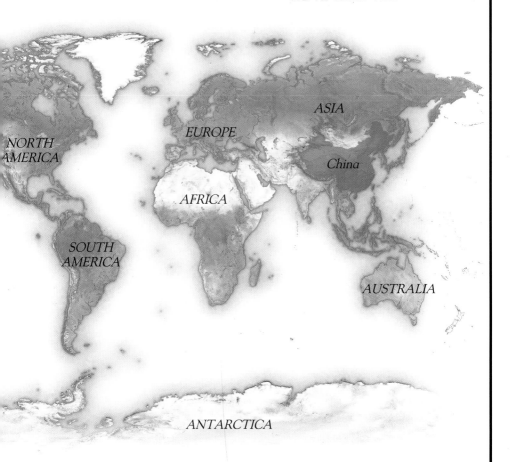

China is on the continent of Asia. It is one of the largest countries in the world, with an area of 3.7 million square miles (9.6 million square km). The Chinese name for the country, Zhōngguó [jung-gwo], means "Middle Kingdom."

Most people in China live along the crowded east coast or near the Yangtze [yang-see] River. Both the Yangtze and the Yellow River cut across China, flowing eastward to the ocean. The rest of the country is mainly covered in deserts, mountains, and highlands. Fewer people live in these areas. The rocky Gobi Desert lies to the north. In the west, there are many mountains, including the world's tallest mountain, Mount Everest. Southern China has an unusual mountain landscape called "karst," with spectacular caves and rock formations.

Yellow River
The Yellow River is 3,400 miles (5,464 km) long. It gets its name from the yellow mud and sand that is carried along by the current.

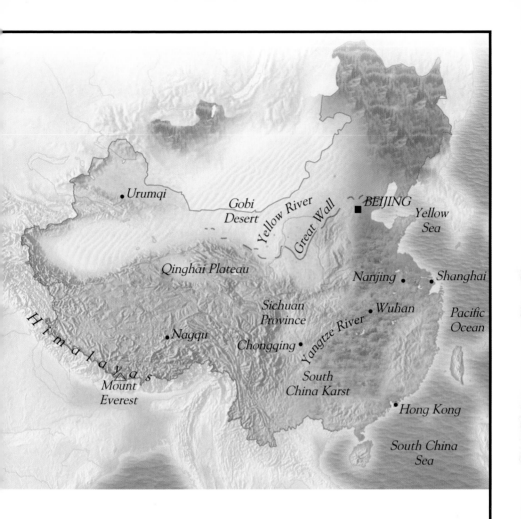

Camels like these provide transportation across the deserts of northern China.

Hills made of limestone rise sharply from the fields of the karst landscape.

More people speak Chinese than any other language. The most common form of Chinese is called Mandarin, but people speak different forms in different parts of the country. The meaning of a word changes depending on how it is said. In Mandarin, the word *shu* [shoo] means "tree" when said with a short, sharp tone. But when it is said with a long, high tone, *shoo* means "book."

Student's workbook

| Hello! | nǐ hǎo
[nee how] | 你好 |

Writing tools

Chinese calligrapher

Instead of an alphabet, Chinese writing uses characters. Each character stands for a word, and they can be added together to make new words. There are thousands of characters. About 2,000 are needed for simple reading and writing.

天	昨天	今天	明天
tiān	zuótiān	jīntiān	míngtiān
[tee-yan]	*[zwo-tee-yan]*	*[jin-tee-yan]*	*[ming-tee-yan]*
day	*yesterday*	*today*	*tomorrow*

Chinese history

The culture of China is at least 4,000 years old, making it the oldest continuous civilization that we know about. Much of Chinese history can be divided into time periods based on dynasties, or royal families.

Timeline

| 2000BCE | 221BCE 207BCE |
| Prehistoric | Qin |

Each dynasty brought its own changes to the country.

During the Qin [chin] Dynasty, China was united by Qin Shi Huang [chin shee hwang], who is known as the first emperor of China. Construction began on the famous Great Wall, designed to protect the northern border of the kingdom, while thousands of clay warriors, called the Terracotta Army, were made to guard the emperor's tomb.

The Terracotta Army

During the Han Dynasty, the Silk Road became an important route for trading goods and ideas between countries of the East and West.

Paper was invented in the Han Dynasty, and the development of printing during the Song Dynasty led to the world's first printed books.

Chinese merchants traded goods made from silk, bronze, and porcelain.

Bronze ornament

Porcelain camel

Silk cloth

Timeline

2000BCE   221BCE 207BCE 220   960   1279

Prehistoric   Qin   Han   Song

The Forbidden City

During the Ming Dynasty, Beijing became the capital of China. A palace complex called the Forbidden City was built for the emperor's family. Ordinary people were not allowed to enter.

In 1911, the Qing [ching] Dynasty was defeated in a revolution, ending the tradition of Chinese emperors.

1368   *1644*   *1911*

     Ming   *Qing*

In 1949, the Communist Party, led by Chairman Mao Zedong [mow zuh-dung], formed the People's Republic of China.

The Communists promised a nation in which everyone would be equal. But Mao made many laws without thinking of the good of the people. Millions starved due to a lack of food. Mao and his Red Guards punished anyone who disagreed with them. China became cut off from the rest of the world.

Mao's Little Red Book
The Little Red Book contains Mao's famous sayings. People carried it with them to prove their loyalty to their leader.

Timeline

2000BCE	221BCE	207BCE	220	960	1279
Prehistoric	Qin	Han		Song	

Chairman Mao at a May Day celebration

Mao died in 1976. Since then, China has raced forward into the modern age, and it is once more open to the rest of the world.

China's Congress meets in the Great Hall of the People in Beijing.

1368	1644	1911	1949
Ming	Qing		Communist

Life in China

With so many people in China, there are not enough resources for everyone. The government limits the population by allowing families to have only one child, or in some cases two. Children are often called "little emperors" because they are so precious, but they also feel great pressure to make their families proud.

Children usually start school at age six. Classes are in Mandarin, but some schools also teach English as a second language. At age 14, students take an important test that is considered the key to a successful future. "Learning is a treasure that will follow its owner everywhere," goes an old Chinese saying.

Friend	péngyou [pung-yoh]	朋友

Traditionally, children in China lived in the same home as their parents, grandparents, and sometimes even their great-grandparents. Today, people move more often, and most homes are small, especially in the crowded cities.

Family and friends often gather for mealtimes. A Chinese meal is made up of many different dishes, which are shared by everyone. These usually include soup, dumplings, steamed and stir-fried dishes, plus plenty of rice or noodles. People use chopsticks to eat.

Noodles

Dumplings

Dim sum

Special foods are served on special occasions. For example, a dish of extra-long noodles on birthdays represents a wish for long life.

Chopsticks

Using chopsticks takes practice. Keep the bottom chopstick still while using the top one to pick up food.

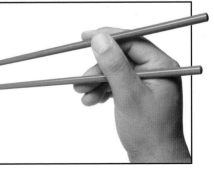

The center of every Chinese town or
city is the busy market. There, people
buy food, household items, clothes, and
other goods. Amid the hustle and bustle,
they can also get a haircut, be fitted
for specially made clothes, have a
foot massage, or see a fortune teller.
The market smells of delicious steamed
buns and echoes with the sounds of
shopkeepers and customers bargaining
over prices.

At the park, people relax. Some gather to practice tai chi [tie chee], an exercise of slow, relaxing movements. Others fly kites or play board games, such as Chinese chess or mah-jongg. Crowds gather around to watch.

Chinese chess

Practicing tai chi in the park

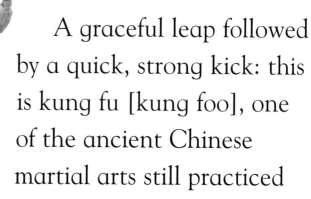

A graceful leap followed by a quick, strong kick: this is kung fu [kung foo], one of the ancient Chinese martial arts still practiced today. It is based on the idea of chi [chee], the energy flow between mind and body.

Many people in China enjoy both traditional and modern pastimes. Other popular sports include gymnastics and ping-pong, as well as basketball, baseball, and soccer.

Ping-pong players in the park

Member of China's Olympic gymnastics team

Chinese opera

China also has a rich tradition of art and music. Many still practice calligraphy, using special brushes for writing characters, and the drama and costumes of Chinese opera have thrilled audiences for more than 1,000 years. These days, modern pop music is becoming more popular, especially among young people.

In the countryside

Only about one-tenth of the land in China can be used for farming. Droughts and floods often make even this land difficult to farm.

Chinese farmers working in waterlogged paddies

More rice grows in China than anywhere else in the world, especially in the warm, wet climate of the south. Rice grows in wet fields called paddies. They may be located on flat river basins or on terraces cut into hillsides. Many farmers wade into the wet paddies to plant the rice seedlings by hand.

Other important crops include wheat, soy beans, sweet potatoes, and many kinds of fruit. In fact, apples were first grown in ancient China.

Soy beans

Sweet potato

Wheat

Rice   mi or mǐfàn
　　　[mee] or [mee-fan]

Wooden homes in a Chinese village

Although more than half of China's population still works on farms, many people are leaving the countryside to move to the cities. Life is often difficult in the country. People can earn more in the city and then send money home to help their families.

Moving to the city usually means living far from home, and perhaps only visiting once a year. In some families, both parents find jobs in the city. Grandparents or other relatives care for the children back in the country.

A grandfather takes his grandson home from school.

Big cities

Chinese cities are very crowded—full of people, buildings, and traffic. The biggest city, Shanghai, has almost 17 million people, including several million residents who live there temporarily for work. The population of Beijing, the capital city, is 14 million.

Shanghai business center

At least 50 cities in China have populations of one million or more.

As more people move to the cities, the cities grow upward and outward. In some cities, too many people have moved in too quickly, and there are not enough homes and jobs for everyone.

Chongqing

More than 30 million people live in the city of Chongqing [chong-ching], and the surrounding area. This very large city is in central China.

Rush hour in Beijing

Ting-a-ling! Once, China was known as a nation of bicycles. Now, the sound heard is "beep-beep" since more people can afford their own cars. However, with millions of new cars on the roads each year, there are massive traffic jams and high levels of pollution.

Maglev train

The Maglev train in Shanghai is one of the fastest trains in the world. It takes less than eight minutes to travel along the 19-mile (30 km) track.

Traditional neighborhoods called "hutongs" [hoo-tongs] are made up of a maze of narrow lanes that lead to courtyards. Homes are arranged around the sides of the courtyards. Due to the rapid growth of cities, many hutongs are being knocked down to make way for modern apartment buildings that can house more people.

People in China usually work six days a week. Many work in factories, making goods that are sold around the world. Factory workers often live in rooms on the factory site. Some factory sites are so big, they are like small cities.

Many people also work at construction sites, helping China's cities expand. New hotels and restaurants are opening all the time, due to the increase in tourism, and they need workers as well.

China's booming economy has helped some people get rich beyond their wildest dreams. Unfortunately, many others still struggle to get by.

Workers in a factory, making electronic goods

The Yangtze

The Chinese name for the Yangtze means "long river." In fact, it is the third longest river in the world. The Yangtze flows 3,900 miles (6,300 km) across the center of China, from the Qinghai [ching-hi] Plateau in the west to the East China Sea near Shanghai.

The Yangtze River Basin is the area that is irrigated by the river. It is ideal land for farming. Along the riverbanks are large cities, such as Chongqing, Wuhan, and Nanjing. Many boats sail along the eastern part of the Yangtze, from Chongqing to the coast.

Traditional fishing nets are often used to catch fish in the Yangtze.

Yangtze   Cháng Jiāng
           [chang jyang]   长江

On the Yangtze, between Chongqing and Wuhan, is the Three Gorges Dam, the biggest dam in the world. This enormous dam prevents flooding in areas downriver and uses river water to generate electricity.

However, to build the dam, an area of spectacular natural beauty was purposely flooded, and entire towns and villages disappeared under the water. Several million people had to move away. The dam has also harmed wildlife and the environment. The Three Gorges Dam has changed the Yangtze forever—both for the better and for the worse.

The Lesser Gorge before the floods raised the water level

Yangtze river dolphin
Experts believe that there
may not be any river dolphins
left in the Yangtze. These
creatures were white and
had long, narrow beaks.

Saving the pandas

What has black-and-white fur and lives in China? Pandas, of course! Sadly, there are not many pandas left. They are an endangered species.

The Chinese word for panda means "bear cat."

Pandas live in forests where they eat bamboo. Much of their habitat has been cleared for farming or building, which means there are now fewer pandas. Animal experts in China are working to increase the panda population. They have set up reserves in Sichuan [sech-wan] Province to protect the remaining panda habitat. They also encourage pandas to have more babies. Slowly, the population is growing again.

Bamboo

Panda	xióngmāo [shyong-mow]	熊猫

Festival time

The Chinese enjoy celebrating. The Chinese calendar begins with the Spring Festival. Also known as the Chinese New Year, it is a noisy, colorful festival that lasts for 15 days.

In China and around the world, families gather for a huge New Year feast that includes special dishes such as jiaozi [jow-zuh], a kind of dumpling. People wear red clothes for luck and hang red decorations. Children receive red packets of lucky money.

Lucky money

Dancers, dressed as dragons or lions, play loud drums to scare away the bad spirits and ensure that the coming year will be a lucky one.

The lion dance performed at a New Year celebration

 On Qing Ming [ching ming], or Clear Brightness Festival, families bring gifts of food to their ancestors' graves.

During the Dragon Boat Festival, boats decorated to look like colorful dragons take part in an exciting race.

People eat dragon-boat dumplings and cheer for their favorite team.

The Midautumn Festival, or Moon Festival, celebrates the harvest. That night, people look up at the full moon and think of loved ones who are far away. They also look for Chang'e [chang-ee], the moon goddess, who is said to live in the moon with a magical rabbit.

Chang'e, the moon goddess

Moon cakes

Friends and relatives give each other moon cakes during the Moon Festival. In ancient China, people hid messages inside these treats.

Modern China

Modern China is constantly changing and its people are always looking toward the future.

One example is the Chinese space program. In 2003, China sent its first astronaut, or taikonaut [tie-ko-naut], into space. Since then, the space program has grown. The main goal of the program is to learn more about the moon and Mars, and China hopes to one day have a permanent base on the moon. In 2007, the Chinese launched an unmanned orbiter to help them study the moon. The orbiter was named *Chang'e 1*, after the moon goddess.

Yang Liwei, China's first taikonaut

Launch of Chang'e 1's *carrier rocket*

The 2008 Olympic Games in Beijing have given the Chinese people the chance to welcome the world to their once-mysterious country. To mark the occasion, they have built high-tech sports arenas, new parks, and better public transportation systems. An effort has also been made to reduce pollution in the capital and other cities through the Green Olympics program.

China's Olympic Stadium is nicknamed the Bird's Nest.

Introduction of the five official 2008 Olympic mascots, whose combined names mean "Welcome to Beijing"

The theme for the Beijing Olympics is "one world, one dream," a sign of how far the country has come. China was once closed off from the rest of the world. Now, it is a proud nation taking its place on the global stage.

Goodbye	zàijiàn	再见
	[zi-jyen]	

Glossary

Ancestors
Family members of past generations.

Ancient
Very old, having existed for many hundreds or thousands of years.

Bamboo
A type of woody grass that grows in tropical places.

Calligraphy
The art of elegant handwriting. In China, calligraphy involves writing characters.

Characters
Symbols that represent words, as used in Chinese writing.

Civilization
The way of life of a people in a particular time and place.

Climate
The typical weather of a place.

Communist Party
The political party that governs China and appoints its leaders.

Congress
A group of government officials that meets to discuss and decide on policies.

Dynasty
A series of rulers from a single family. Periods of Chinese history are often identified by the ruling dynasty.

Emperor
The ruler of an empire or country. Chinese emperors had complete authority over their subjects.

Highlands
An area of land at a high altitude, which is often hilly or mountainous.

Irrigate
To supply farmland with water using canals, channels, or some other man-made system.

Karst
A landscape of mountains and caves formed from limestone rock.

Mandarin
The official language of China.

Martial arts
Styles of fighting, such as kung fu, karate, or judo, which are often practiced as sports.

Minority
A small group of people with different traits than most of the people in their country.

Orbiter
A spacecraft that circles around a moon or planet.

Population
The number of people who live in a place.

Silk Road
A historical trade route that led from southern Europe to China, passing through Arabia, Egypt, Persia, and India along the way.

Tone
The highness or lowness of a sound. Four tones are used to speak Mandarin.